THE SHIPWRIGHT AND THE SCHOONER

Building a Windjammer in the New England Tradition

HAROLD BURNHAM

Photographs by DAN TOBYNE

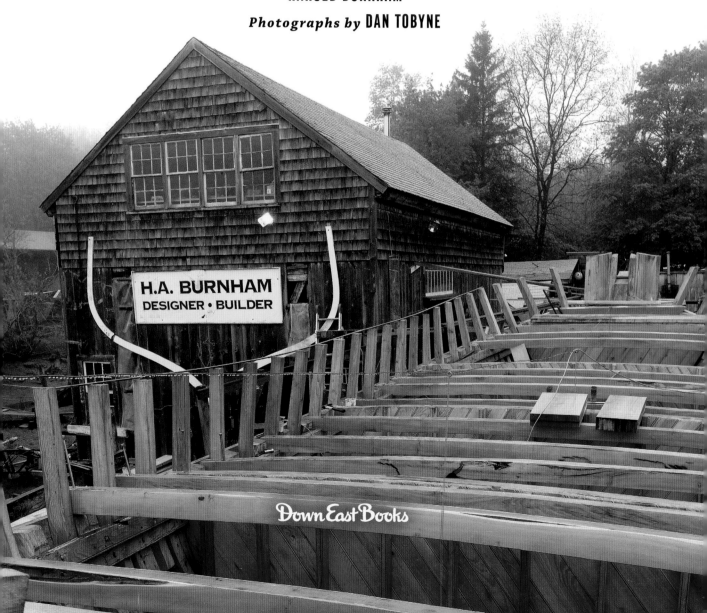

DownEast Books

Published by Down East Books
An imprint of Globe Pequot
Trade division of The Rowman & Littlefield Publishing Group, Inc.
4501 Forbes Boulevard, Suite 200, Lanham, Maryland 20706
www.rowman.com

Unit A, Whitacre Mews, 26-34 Stannary Street, London SE11 4AB, United Kingdom

Distributed by NATIONAL BOOK NETWORK

Designed by Lynda Chilton, Chilton Creative

Text copyright © 2016 by Harold Burnham
Photographs © 2016 by Dan Tobyne

British Library Cataloguing in Publication Information Available

Library of Congress Cataloging-in-Publication Data

Library of Congress Cataloging-in-Publication Data Available

ISBN 978-1-60893-462-1 (paper : alk. paper)
ISBN 978-1-60893-463-8 (electronic)

∞™ The paper used in this publication meets the minimum requirements of American National Standard for Information Sciences—Permanence of Paper for Printed Library Materials, ANSI/NISO Z39.48-1992.

Printed in the United States of America

Contents

Foreword

The smell is what I remember most about my first visit to the boatyard. The tide was out that hot August night, and the fusty smell of mudflats blended with whiffs of turpentine and cut wood. My daughter and I had come to meet Harold Burnham, the shipwright and owner, to talk about photographing the construction of his new schooner.

Harold, a master shipwright, builds boats using the materials and methods of his ancestors. He is keeping a tradition alive in a small New England town where, over the past four centuries, an estimated 4,000 wooden ships were built.

As the story goes, a man named Thomas Burnham built the first boat in Essex around 1650. He built the boat in his house and come spring, had to tear a wall out to get the boat down to the river.

Harold wouldn't be tearing out any walls in his house. His boat would come together outside, open to the weather, and if inside work was needed, he'd use the barn his father had rebuilt on the foundation of the old shop.

Entering the boatyard we could make out a number of structures, including a house at the top of the rise, and a barn below. We headed for the barn, largest of the buildings, and closest to the water's edge. It was dark out, with little lighting, and as we made our way down, we navigated many obstacles: coils of rope, nautical gear, stacks of wood, a couple of old boats on jack stands, and a strange gangway that ran past the building and down toward the river. Inside, the barn was expansive, high-ceilinged, and open, with a workbench running the length of one wall, and a large collection of half models on the other. The interior was illuminated by two dim ceiling lights, and we could just make out an old dory hanging from the rafters, and what seemed like an acre of heavily stained floorboards that trailed off into darkness. Steep, tight stairs ran up one wall, and light escaping through a hatchway gave birth to muted wall shadows and an eerie impression of a half-model sailing fleet. We moved toward the stairs, and as we ascended, we began to hear the muffled sound of voices.

Upon entering the loft the sight left us speechless. A woodstove was attached to the ceiling by long metal rods, and every inch of space around the perimeter was stuffed with nautical equipment—shelves of rigging, sail-making hardware, spools of thread, blocks and tackle, and racks of plans. A bench in the corner harbored what looked like drawings, and on the floor you could see that the lines for the new boat had been "lofted" (drawn, full scale), in an assortment of colors.

Scattered about were all sorts of tools: awls, long thin strips of wood, strange flexible measuring devices, odd-shaped weights, and an assortment of rules. A sewing machine sat off to one side, along with a band saw, bolts of sailcloth, a rocking chair, and a couch. The loft had a very low ceiling, but as I would soon find out, most work in that part of the barn takes place on the floor.

It was here that we also found Harold. He was pondering an issue involving degrees of curvature for one of the lines. He paused for a few seconds as he looked over at us, and in what I was to learn later was typical Harold fashion, stared at us for a moment before slowly lowering his head back down to continue his discussion with the other men in the room. They were throwing around words like *dead-rise* and *futtocks, fairings* and *offsets,* and other words I could only assume referred to the more-technical aspects of boatbuilding.

After about five minutes he looked up and said, "Hi, I'm Harold." and that was the beginning of a grand adventure, and one of the most interesting years of my life.

~ Dan Tobyne

Chuck Redman and Harold making patterns for the stem rabbit. Inset: The workbench.

Introduction

The design process for the *Ardelle* started in August of 2009, and continued as time allowed through July of 2010, when the vessel was lofted. While building and owning a vessel may have been something I dreamed about, until that point it wasn't something I'd planned. Forget about it not being plan A; it wasn't even plan B.

Plan A was for someone else to hire me to build a boat, and plan B was for someone to hire me to practice one of my other talents. Building the *Ardelle* was definitely plan C, but since A and B weren't keeping me busy, I went with C, and the more I thought about it, the more I realized there were good reasons to start. First, I felt I couldn't afford to waste time trying to fix my old boat, the *Maine*. It needed too much work. And since I was going to work for free, it might as well be on building a new boat, as opposed to repairing an old one. And second, I felt it would be nice for my kids to see the family shipyard run once more while they were still living at home.

The process started slowly, but in between other jobs, the plan grew, and although I was still hoping to build a boat with someone else's money, it looked more and more like I was building one with my own.

~Harold Burnham

The Ardelle's keel lying on the bedding timbers before construction began.

1

The Beginning

My friend Richard Osborn says, "You feel most alive when you're terrified out of your mind," and so it was that I found myself, on a warm September day, in front of a crowd of family, friends, and well-wishers, all expecting me to say something interesting about the forty-ton vessel I was about to build.

This wasn't the first time I'd built a boat like this. Since 1994, when I'd given up my seagoing career, I've been lucky enough to make the lion's share of my livelihood by building and repairing wooden boats in the winter. During the summer months, I run a small charter business.

The boats I design and build are, for the most part, representations of historic, indigenous vessels. I control the costs by purchasing raw materials and fabricating as many components of the boat as possible myself, or with a talented gang of craftsmen who are as passionate as I am about preserving the traditions of Essex shipbuilding. In spite of that, by the spring of 2010, I hadn't had an order for a boat in five years. I was ready for a new project, having gathered the logs, hardware, fasteners, line, rigging, and sailcloth, and knowing I could salvage most of what I didn't have from my old schooner, the *Maine*. With no customers on the horizon, it seemed like the only sensible way out of the boatbuilding business was to build a boat. It was my hope that with the income from a new Coast Guard inspected vessel for my charter business, I could keep my family and the boat building business going until the next customer showed up.

Even though I'd collected most of the materials, I knew that I couldn't build the boat alone in one winter. Further complicating matters was the fact that I didn't have the resources to pay anyone to help me do it. While starting a project in this sort of predicament might seem audacious, it was actually an act of utter desperation. The small financial ledge I was standing on was quickly crumbling.

My friend and customer, Tom Ellis, did the introduction for me that day. Fifteen years earlier he'd hired me to build an even larger vessel than the one I was about to start. As I stood there, I thought of what he'd said to me when I told him that he probably didn't have the money he needed to build his boat: "I might not have enough money, but I have friends." So, as I looked out at the group of four hundred or more people that had come to help and support me, I realized I was truly blessed and that this dream of mine might actually stand a chance.

There were many times during construction when I wondered if I'd ever be able to finish the project, or what I'd been thinking when I decided to start it in the first place—only to be interrupted by someone wandering into the yard, looking for a way to help out. One of those friends was Dan Tobyne. Like John Clayton, Lew Joslyn, and many others before him, Dan was drawn to the Essex River Basin to photograph wooden ships under construction. Born in Beverly, Massachusetts, Dan loves the sea and all it stands for—in his words, "romance, intrigue, history, and adventure." One of his ancestors was a ship's captain who sailed an Essex-built schooner, and Dan had heard his stories as a child.

Chuck's (Harold's father) canoe and Aunt Mary's boat hanging in the barn. Mary's boat was built by Nelson Lane in Ipswich, Mass., in the 1930s and is the last known to exist of a type once ubiquitous in Essex.

Throughout his life, Dan has worn many different hats, working in the building trades, as a teacher and outdoor-education instructor with troubled youth, and as the director of a program for high-school dropouts. His passions include the outdoors and photography, and he's the author and photographer of several books. He'd been looking for a boatbuilding project to photograph when we started work on the *Ardelle*.

Dan not only photographed the boat under construction—he also lived and breathed the project from beginning to end, becoming a real member of the crew. He shared in the entire experience, and was around the shipyard so often that his initial

Left: Autumn colors make a great back-drop for the Ardelle in frame.

At this point the stem, sternpost, and several frames are stood up on the keel, in addition to the bulkhead separating the main hold from the aft cabin.

Right: Preparing the Ardelle for launch, July 9, 2011.

promise to me rang true. He blended into the background and became part of the fabric, allowing everyone else to become comfortable with his camera. We seldom noticed him perched above, or lying beneath, shooting the shipwrights and their work at what he felt was the best angle. Like everyone else, he gave *Ardelle* his best talents.

We launched the *Ardelle* into the tide on July 9, and received our Coast Guard certification on September 2, the day before the 2011 Gloucester Schooner Festival. Completing her in just under a year was an amazing effort, and I will be eternally grateful to Dan for recording the process.

2

Essex

Whomen you look at the village of Essex, Massachusetts, today it's difficult to imagine that this backwater town located in the middle of an expansive salt marsh was once a major shipbuilding center.

Boatbuilding started in Essex shortly after it was settled in 1635. It was an ideal location to build boats, owing to a local abundance of good ship timber and its proximity to rich offshore fishing grounds. Recognizing the economic importance of the shipbuilding industry to the town, in 1668 the town fathers set aside an acre of land along the river to "build ships and employ workmen to that end." The concept of a municipal shipyard seems unique to Essex and the result of its creation was incredibly fruitful. Although there were many shipyards scattered along the river in Essex, the town's shipbuilding property was amongst the most productive. The land was used continuously for nearly three centuries. I used it to build two vessels in 1997 and 1998 and it is kept open for shipbuilding to this very day.

Until 1819, Essex was known as the Chebacco Parish of Ipswich, Massachusetts. In the eighteenth century, locally built Chebacco boats developed a well-earned reputation for quality construction. They were built in large numbers and the standard vessel types that evolved were used in nearby Gloucester, Massachusetts and along the Atlantic coast. In the mid-nineteenth century when Gloucester became

world famous for its fast and able fishing schooners, Essex became known as the town that built them.

After World War II, ship's timber became increasingly scarce and vessels built of other materials began filling the voids in the fishing fleet. The building of large wooden vessels became a thing of the past. Moreover, as all that was required to build a wooden ship was a few hand tools, a pile of timber, and a group of people who knew how to craft it, once the vessels sailed away the industry disappeared, and the town began to lose an important part of its identity.

Over the next decades, the town became far better known for its many antique shops, tourism, and seafood, but its rich history of shipbuilding did not die out altogether. Essex shipbuilding lived on in books, photographs, models, tools, and artifacts. It also lived on in our vessels, which continue to ply the waters of the world. Despite the enormous cost, several Essex-built fishing schooners have been rebuilt and designated as National Historic Landmarks. They serve as roving ambassadors to our national heritage and of the little town that created them. Most importantly, albeit away from the water's edge, out of sight, and no longer on an industrial scale, a number of boats continued to be built in Essex. The Essex Shipbuilding Muse-ums carefully kept vessel lists reflect this. From 1860 up until the year 2000, there were only five years in which no vessels were built in Essex and none of those years were consecutive.

The person who built the most boats in Essex during my upbringing was Brad Story. Brad, a sixth generation boat builder, started building boats in his father's yard in the early 1970s. He and his gang built fifty-two of them. Brad's shop was located between my parent's house and my family's ship-yard and throughout much of my childhood and early adult life, I frequently spent time there. There is something alluring about seeing a boat under construc-tion, and many others would stop by the yard as well. Some of us probably spent far too much time hanging around. I'm thankful that

Zack and Harold nail a spruce sapling atop the sternpost to celebrate comple-tion of the frame.

Brad was patient with us. I respected the fact that when his shop door was closed and locked from the inside, it probably meant he didn't want company. I'm not sure that everyone got the hint.

When I started building and repairing boats, there were many times I felt the same frustration that Brad must have felt, and being a traditionalist, I tried the same techniques he had used to keep the curious at bay. The barricades at the doors and windows didn't work, and although disappearing was effective at getting people to leave, it didn't help me meet my deadlines, and oftentimes my "visitors" would just come back. Eventually I decided that anytime a visitor stopped by, I would give them a few minutes to look around and, if they persisted in staying, I would put them to work.

Interestingly, they usually did what I asked and came back for more. I found myself saving up tasks in case someone showed up, and as launchings approached, I found I was often managing the crew rather than building the boat. I assumed the novelty would wear off as I became more professional. I found it strange for someone to show up and work for nothing on a boat a customer was paying me to work on. I was surprised to learn that it didn't seem to matter.

There are many people who love Essex and are committed to keeping our heritage of wooden boatbuilding alive. Some of these do it by building boats and others contribute in different ways. In 1976, the Essex Historical Society opened the Essex Shipbuilding Museum. Housed in an old schoolhouse, the museum's collections included old ship-building tools, artifacts, and models of Essex-built schooners on loan from the Smithsonian.

In 1989, Captain Bob Douglas stopped by the museum as a gang was involved in recreating the keel, keelson, and several frame sections of one of our schooners to be installed as an exhibit. A short time later, Bob called the museum to tell them that they didn't need to continue work on the schooner exhibit. He and Brian Duffy had raised the entire hulk of the Essex-built schooner *Evelina M. Goulart* off of the bottom of Fairhaven Harbor and were planning to tow it to Essex as a gift to the museum. The fact that the Goulart was ninety-two feet long, twenty-two feet wide, drew twelve feet of water, and weighed two hundred and fifty tons cannot start to explain the absurdity of this "gift." Even more absurd is the fact that the museum accepted it and it all worked out for the best.

In the autumn of 1990 the *Evelina M. Goulart* returned to Essex and she was hauled onto the land the town fathers had set aside for shipbuilding. The energy generated by the project helped the museum to purchase the adjacent property, formerly the Story Shipyard and helped inspire Tom Ellis to have a new schooner built in 1996.

Brad was Tom's first choice as builder but as he had already been commissioned to build a lobster boat that winter, so Brad decided to send Tom to me. Tom's not

the kind of guy who takes no for an answer and while I never told him I could do the job, how much it would cost, or how long it would take, he hired me without giving it a second thought. We cut the first trees in September, laid the keel in December, launched her in June, and in July, the Schooner *Thomas E. Lannon* ran her first charter. Most people marveled at the way the *Lannon* came together, but thinking back on it often gives me nightmares. At the time, I was only twenty-nine years old, the *Lannon* was the first heavily constructed vessel built in Essex in forty-eight years, and I had become the designer by default.

The successful construction of the *Lannon* helped to pave the way for my building several other vessels. The Chebacco boat *Lewis H. Story* was commissioned by the Shipbuilding Museum and was launched in 1998. Next was the Chebacco Schooner *Fame* launched in 2003 followed by the Schooner *Isabella* launched in 2006.

Over the years following the building of the *Isabella* I had the opportunity to work on some interesting restoration projects, but continued to cut and season timber in anticipation of another boatbuilding contract, or for restoration work on my own boat, the pinky *Maine*.

The contract never came and the deciding moment for the *Maine* came in the spring of 2009. While careening her on to a beach for painting, I noticed something on one of the forward planks that didn't look right. I gave the spot a rap with my broom, and the handle went straight through the bottom of the boat! While I was able to quickly patch her up before the tide came in, and continued to sail her, my thoughts of restoring the *Maine* were over. I needed a new boat and with the yard, the equipment, and the material available to me, I decided that there was no time like the present.

Chuck R. working at the drafting table in the mold loft

Inset: An early sketch of the Ardelle's construction

3

Design

The shape of a wooden vessel is traditionally derived from a scale half model. This type of model represents one side or one half of the finished hull. As boats are symmetrical, the other side of the vessel is a mirror image of the one the model represents. Half models are cut or carved out of a block of wood, and usually made up of layers known as lifts. A half-inch-scale model is often made using half-inch lifts so that each lift represents a horizontal cut through the hull one foot thick.

Once completed, a shipwright can trace the profile (or side view) of the vessel and then take the model apart and trace each of the lifts to quickly produce a half-breath plan (or top view), which looks a lot like a topographical map of the hull. Then by drawing perpendicular lines known as stations through the half-breath plan and profile plans along the length of the drawings and plotting the widths of the half breaths at their proper heights, a sectional plan (or head-on view) can be developed.

Finally, a table of offsets can be created, that will be used in the process known as lofting—in layman's terms, drawing the vessel's lines, full scale, on the floor. This process allows full-size patterns and molds to be built that shipwrights can then use to build the vessel.

If someone has a set of lines for a boat, they can also make a good half model of her very quickly by tracing the lines on the lifts, cutting them out, putting them together, and fairing them off. Making models is something I started doing as a boy, and in my lifetime I've made hundreds of them. Building models has not only helped me to design boats, it's also given me an intuitive sense of how hulls interact with the water under different conditions. Once I know what I want, it only takes me an hour or so to make a good working model that can be used to trace a set of lines. This takes far less time than it would for me to draw the lines using battens and curves, and it's one of the reasons I like this method.

Another reason I prefer a model to a drawing is that anyone can look at a model and, with no training, or drafting skills, know instantly what the finished hull will look like.

In August of 2009, without knowing exactly what I wanted for a new boat, or how I'd pay for it, I started the design process by carving two models. The first model was of my old schooner, *Maine*. I knew her form well, and had sailed her in all sorts of weather conditions, so it seemed prudent that before I started making any changes, I ought to have her model in front of me as a starting point. Once I finished that model, I carved another that incorporated changes I believed would be improvements. I added some freeboard for reserve buoyancy, and a little beam for stability.

I liked Ebenezer Burnham's pinky schooner *Maine*, built in Essex, Massachusetts, in 1845, and at the time intended to keep the name "*Maine*" for the new boat. I decided to rake the new model's stem out, making its bow less bluff, and easier to plank, but I kept the overall length of the rig about the same as my old *Maine*, allowing me to use her spars and standing rigging. The most important difference between the old *Maine* and the new vessel would be meeting the requirements for Coast Guard inspection, which would allow her to carry more than six passengers. At that point, I wasn't sure how many people I wanted to carry.

Sometime before Christmas I traced my model, and sent the lines of the improved design with a few frames added, along with sketches of the arrangement and sail plan, to my friend, David Wyman. I also sent him the business plan, which stated I wanted to carry 49 passengers. David suggested that for my plan to work I needed to build a bigger boat.

I went back to my models and at the end of March, I sent him the lines and sketches of a much larger vessel. At this point I began to realize that the boat had changed so much, it needed a new name. I decided to name her *Ardelle*, after my paternal grandmother. She lived at the boatyard when I was a boy, and instilled in me many of the values I have today.

This wall in the shop is almost completely covered with half models made by Harold and his father. Some of these are original designs and others were made of boats they admired or worked on.

John Abizaid of Mayer tree service unloading white oak logs at the mill.

Inset: It is said that, "to a friendship each year adds a ring, as to an oak."

The Wood and the Mill

WOOD

Sourcing good shipbuilding material is only slightly less difficult than finding customers. This is one of the reasons we run our own mill. When we built the *Lannon*, Tom Ellis was able to convince people to allow us to make selective cuts of timber on both conservation lands and private property. Thus began our practice of using mostly local timber in our boats. Building the *Lannon*, we contracted with sawyer Tony Chaplick who used his portable sawmill to cut the timber. When Tony moved away, he offered to sell me his mill. At the time it felt as if I could not stay in business without it. Now, not only has the mill become integral to our shipyard, operating it is one of my favorite parts of building a boat.

Most of the logs I used in *Ardelle* came from my friend Dan Mayer's tree service based in Essex—more specifically, from his brother-in-law John Abazaid. John sells me the discarded white pine, white oak, and locust left over from land clearing, estate-work, and residential projects, allowing me to claim that our vessels are almost entirely made from "recycled" material. Really though, this has as much to do with Yankee thrift as it does with any green initiative we might talk about.

Because it comes from a living thing, there is something sacred about working with wood. Completing the whole process from stump to ship makes me feel connected to something much larger than myself. It is as if the boat is created through me and that my work is just part of an organic process by which every piece of wood finds its natural place in the vessel and nothing is wasted. The slabs and scraps are used for fuel to heat the house, the loft, and the steam box. The chips are used to bed down horses, and sawdust and ashes go into my grandfather's raspberry patch. If I am not lost at sea, I hope my ashes will someday join that patch as well.

The primary wood I used in the *Ardelle* was white oak. It's a wonderful material, and while it's one of the toughest woods available, when green, it can be cut like a piece of cheese with an adze. It can be heated and bent in ways that are hard to imagine, and when cooled, holds its shape. White oak is also less prone to rot than its cousin, the red oak, and if kept dry or immersed in salt water, it can last indefinitely. White oak can be used for just about anything below the waterline, and when you're looking for something strong and rigid, and you're not concerned about weight, it's one of the best woods there is. White oak does have a few drawbacks: It can be difficult to machine, it doesn't hold paint well, and it doesn't glue at all.

I also used a lot of white pine in *Ardelle*. I know pine has a reputation for rotting, but that is only because people use the sapwood in places where they should not. I use the sapwood for stage planks or building sheds, keeping only the heartwood for the vessels. Pine is not as tough as oak, but that's one of its attributes. It's much lighter, a wonderful material to carve, holds glue well, and has some natural give to it. You have to drill a piece of oak for just about every fastening, whereas with pine, you can drive a nail or screw with ease. I use pine for half models, battens, blocking, staging, decking, trunks, bulkheads, bulwarks, mast wedges, interior joinery, and planking on small boats.

I also used black locust in the *Ardelle*. Locust is harder to work with than pine or oak and although it's as strong as oak, it isn't as tough. It is, however, more dimensionally stable than oak, and incredibly rot-resistant. Locust is the best material for trunnels—tree nails used to hold the boat together—because it drives easier, and lasts longer than the material it passes through. Locust can usually be used interchangeably with oak and there are several places I prefer to use it. It's the best timber for the parts of the boat prone to shrinking, swelling, and rot, such as the stanchions supporting the bulwarks and those parts of the boat that will remain half-submersed, such as the stem and rudder.

Harold changing blades on the mill after finding some pieces of iron buried in the log.

I used other woods in *Ardelle*, including spruce for spars, and cherry for dressing up the interior. I used to use a lot more tropical hardwoods than I do now, but they are more expensive than they used to be, and the mill has made using them unnecessary. Besides, it would be hard to claim I build indigenous vessels if I used woods from Africa and South America.

Chuck Redman discussing something with Harold as he cuts frame stock on the mill.

Running the mill takes a lot of concentration. Harold generally preferred to do the milling at times when the gang was not around.

Bernie Power (on the feed side) and Chuck R. planing pine for the Ardelle's *watertight bulkheads.*

MILLING

There's a general order to how I mill wood, and by the time a log is properly positioned on the mill bed, I've rolled it over a number of times, both on the platform and in my mind. I know what I need for timber and try to "read" each log as best I can. If all goes well the logs, maximum potential will find its way into the boat.

Large-girthed oak logs will likely become keels and deadwood, and longer, thinner stock usually makes good planking material. Shorter stock with crotches or bells will often be made into frame stock, or the all-important compass timber.

Beyond looking at the size and shape of a log and places where limbs might have once protruded, I also look at the bark for clues as to what lies underneath. Bumps and swirls often indicate knots or gnarly wood. Long folds might indicate a lightning strike, and in the case of locust, you can sometimes see holes indicating ants. Metal sticking out of any log is always a bad sign. I also look at the butt ends of each log for telltale blue stains, indicating that iron is lurking someplace inside.

There are other things on the end of a log I look for as well. If a tree was windshook, the ring shakes will often show, and if the tree burned at any point, you will often see a brown ring in the grain. The wood often falls apart at these spots. If the tree was improperly felled, you can sometimes see holes where the grain's been pulled out of the hinge. This may not sound like much of a problem, but I've seen some pull-outs run four feet into the butt end of an otherwise-perfect log.

With any luck things go smoothly, and I can cut the pieces I'd hoped for out of the log I hoped to get them out of. That's not always the case. Sometimes milling exposes hidden defects in a log or worse yet, iron. In our sawmill shed we keep a small museum of nails, spikes, screws, eyebolts, barbed wire, clothesline pulleys, metal signs, and cables that had to be worked around. Every piece in the collection destroyed at least one of our saw blades.

The parts of the boat that are above the waterline—the planking, top timbers, stanchions, deck beams, and all the pine stock—are best air-dried. As the scantling thickness of these timbers is about the same for vessels from forty to sixty-five feet, these can be cut and stored under cover for a long time. I generally cut and dry these timbers first.

I have two drying sheds. The first shed, and the one nearest the mill, is where I generally store oak planking. I've learned to be very careful about what I place in the sheds. There's a lot of wood-moving involved in boatbuilding, and there's no point in constantly moving around what you aren't going to use.

While the two-inch planks are still on the mill bed, I give them a careful looking over with an understanding of what I'll need for planking stock, and where best to use the different pieces on the boat. Wider, flat-sawn boards will fill in the bottom of the boat, where they will always remain wet. Narrower, more stable boards with a vertical grain will be used above the waterline, where they'll be subject to wind and weather. If there's pith in a plank, the first thing I do is saw the plank in two pieces, down the length of the pith, with a circular saw. If I don't, it will check. I next cut the sapwood off of the planks, and finally, I roll the planks off the mill into the first drying shed.

Pine is dried in the second shed. This stock is generally cut square-edged, with the sapwood and pith removed. Because it's lighter and easier to move, we usually stick it on sleepers in the second shed.

Wood that doesn't require drying is usually stored in the creek underwater or cut not long before we start construction. In the case of the compass timber and frame stock, we generally sticker it in the shade until just before we need it and then it is spread out over every inch of the yard so that we can pick it over one piece at a time.

With the *Ardelle*, when the planking and pine sheds were full, and every inch of the yard was covered with two or three layers of flitch, I had most of the stock I needed and it was time to start building.

Chuck cutting a frame futtock on the vertical band saw.

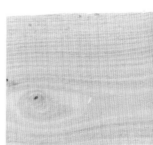

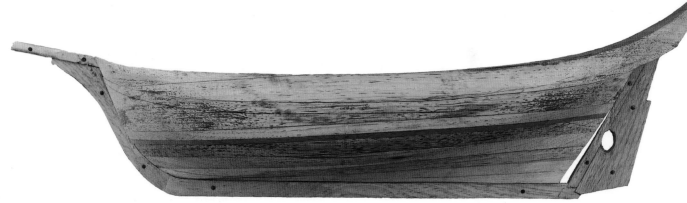

5

The Loft and Lofting

As I mentioned in my section on design, before we could start building the *Ardelle*, she had to be lofted. This work was done in the loft above the shop in the barn, which, in addition to being used as our "mold loft," is also used as our "sail loft" and "rigging loft."

The process of lofting involves drawing the profile, half-breath and sectional views of the vessel full scale and checking them against one another to ensure that the hull is fair. Because our loft floor measures only forty feet by sixteen feet and the *Ardelle* is fifty-eight feet long, we had to loft the vessel in two sections. This made for a lot of lines to keep track of and required a lot of different colored pencils and careful and detailed labeling. Lofting is tedious and intense work, and I prefer to get it done as quickly as possible, so once the floor was painted and the grid laid down, I worked non-stop for a week to get the boat lofted.

About this time a man showed up looking for advice. He was thinking about going to a boatbuilding school and wanted to know what I thought of the school he was interested in. I asked if he'd put a deposit down yet and he answered no, but he was determined to spend the rest of his working years doing something he loved.

I took a liking to him, and told him if he would help with *Ardelle* he could work as many hours as he wanted, come and go as he pleased, and quit anytime. I also

Left: When the wood is dark from age or wet,46 a race knife is used to mark out the futtocks.

Right: Sometimes two or three frames are molded out at the same time.

Below: Cutting futtocks on the band saw.

mentioned that I'd teach him as much as I could. He left with a decision to make: He could either go to school, or build a boat.

Chuck Redman started in the loft the next day.

I'd lofted the boat before he started, but I always appreciate a second opinion, so his first job was to check my work. Using the tick sticks and battens, he went over every line and found a few spots that needed some adjusting. Then, as we had both done some adjusting, he pulled a new set of offsets and made a scaled drawing of the lofted vessel from which we both carved half models to satisfy ourselves that we'd know exactly what the finished boat would look like.

With that done, Chuck began lifting the lines and making patterns and molds. Patterns are used to develop the shapes and parts of the centerline structure, and

are for the most part lifted from the profile plan. Molds, on the other hand, are used to develop the shapes of frames and are lifted from the sectional view.

An experienced loftsman can produce about three or four molds a day, but because we kept Chuck working on other things, it took him a bit longer. When he finished the molds and patterns, Chuck put some of his other skills to work up in the loft building sails for both the *Ardelle* and the *Fame*. This truly made the loft Chuck's domain throughout most of the construction of *Ardelle*.

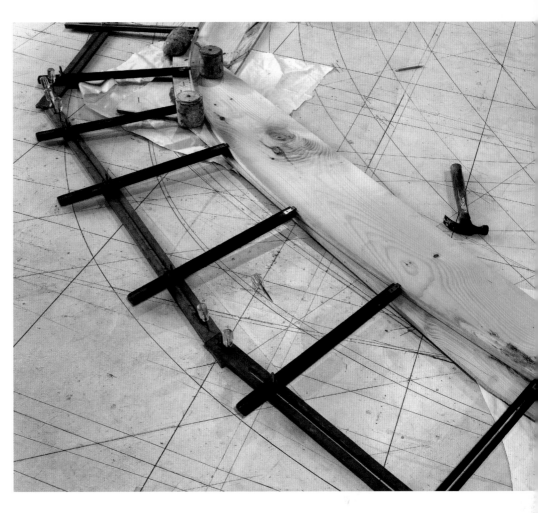

Left: Chuck R. and I working out a detail on the mold. Note the body plan on the floor in the foreground, the trammel, the battens hung on the wall to the right, and the couch with guitar by the window.

Above: The trammel being held in place by awls and used to "lift" the line from the body plan drawn on the floor and transfer it to the mold.

Zack up in the loft laying out the hole for the shaft log. The propeller shaft and stuffing box are beside him on the floor.

"Frame up!" was called out and up it went, the first of Ardelle's frames.

6

Laying the Keel and Framing

Beyond the fact that she was built out in the open where everyone could see her come together, part of what made the *Ardelle's* construction noteworthy is that we built her using traditional heavy construction techniques. These techniques involve the use of double-sawn frames and trunnel fastenings, both of which are rarely used today.

As trees generally do not grow in the shape of a hull there are two ways to make the frames (or ribs) for a round-bottomed wooden vessel. To get the appropriate shapes for the hull, a shipwright can either bend the frame into a form using straight-grained timber, or saw out the shape of the frame from a number of pieces of crooked wood, as we did for the *Ardelle*. In *Ardelle's* case, rather than trying to make fancy joints to hold all the pieces together, we simply doubled up the pieces of wood and staggered the joints. Thus this technique is called "double sawn framing."

While bent frames have the advantage of having their grain follow the shape of the vessel, sawn frames don't have to be bent, so they can be made much heavier, which is why they were used for commercial construction. Heavy construction also allows for trunnel fastenings to be used in the vessel. A trunnel (properly spelled treenail) is a wooden fastening not unlike the pegs that hold furniture together. Because they are not susceptible to oxidation or corrosion, trunnels are generally accepted as a superior fastening for wooden vessels. For reasons of both strength and mechanical bond, however, trunnels must be made proportionately much larger than fastenings made of metal. Therefore trunnels are generally not used in boats built with bent frames or light construction techniques. If trunnels were used in this type of vessel the holes that were drilled to insert them would be so large as to weaken the overall structure of the vessel.

While vessels continued to be built in Essex after World War II, most of the boats constructed in this period were built using light construction techniques and the use of trunnels was abandoned altogether. That is, up until we built the *Lannon* in 1997. Because of the *Lannon*'s size and historic nature, we used traditional heavy construction techniques. Looking back I feel very lucky that Tom Ellis hired me to build that vessel when he did. At that time there were still a few people around that could tell us how to build a boat using the old methods. Since then, especially as those people are now gone, I feel it is important to involve as many people as I can in what I do, in the hope that the skills will live on. I will try to describe the procedure below.

First, Steve Willard, Zack, and I used the patterns Chuck had lofted to build the keel structure out of a number of long pieces of oak which we scarfed together and into a seven-thousand pound chunk of lead. After the keel scarfs were fit we bolted the structure together and set it up like a backbone by the river's edge. The next step was to use the molds to build the frames or ribs. The molds were taken from the loft out into the yard where the frame stock was spread basically everywhere and used to mark out the futtocks or smaller parts that would be pieced together to form the frames. This process is called molding the timber, and how well it is done directly impacts a vessel's strength and longevity. To do this well, the person molding the timber had to have a thorough knowledge of the vessel's shape and a mental picture of all the available timber, making sure that each piece found its correct place within the vessel's frame.

As the futtocks were laid out on the timber. each one had to be carefully marked and labeled in order to prevent us

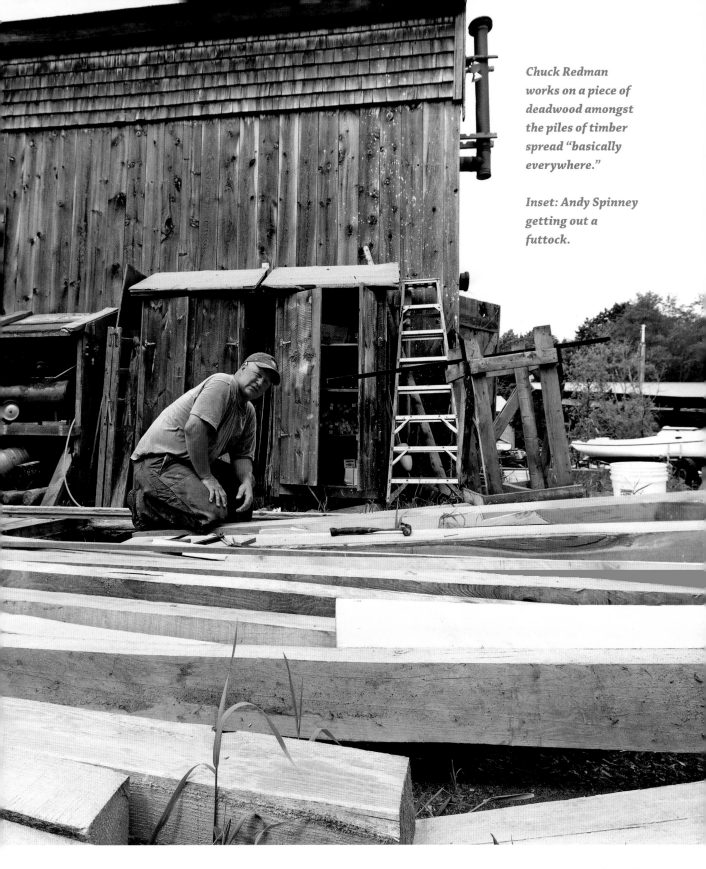

Chuck Redman works on a piece of deadwood amongst the piles of timber spread "basically everywhere."

Inset: Andy Spinney getting out a futtock.

from spending a lot of time turning invaluable compass timber into firewood. After we traced a mold on the wood we marked the frame number, followed by the section of the frame the futtock was part of. Along with this information an arrow was drawn, indicating which way the futtock should be fed into the band saw so that the bevels would go in the right direction. Finally, the bevel angles needed to be marked out so that each ever-changing degree of bevel on the face of the frame could be cut accordingly. When all the pieces for any particular frame had been molded they were then moved to the band saw. The sawyer then carefully cut them out while simultaneously the beveller tilted the table. If the sawyer and beveller did not coordinate their efforts, the blade of the saw would bind and make everything more difficult. When a few helpers jumped in to support the heavy timbers at steep angles, it made the process all the more interesting. Some have compared this work to making music in that it is something creative that requires multiple skilled people to time their efforts in order to produce a quality product.

After all the futtocks for any particular frame were cut out, the faying surfaces were joined so that they fit tightly together. The frames were then assembled on the shop floor. The first step in this process was to put the forward floor (the lower futtock that crosses the keel) on blocks, to elevate it and then to dog it down. Pinch dogs or "dogs" resemble huge staples, one end of which was driven into the futtock and the other into the shop floor to keep the futtock from moving.

After the forward floor was dogged down, we drove a single nail through the centerline of the mold and into the centerline of the floor. Then we used the mold to mark and cut the ends of each of the forward futtocks on that side of the boat, blocking and dogging them in place as we went. Next we pulled the nail, flipped the mold over, and drove the nail back through the same hole in the mold and into the same hole in the floor. Again we used the mold to cut, assemble, and dog down the forward futtocks on the other side of the frame, checking to see

*The tide is just part of daily life on the edge of the salt marsh.
Harold and his team worked both with it and around it. Here,
Zack, Chuck, Steve, and Harold are installing Ardelle's last
few forward cant frames with water lapping up around them.*

Chuck R., Zack, and Steve (inside) hoisting a cant frame up onto the rib band and into its notch.

Inset: Chuck R. and Harold clamping a rib band onto the frames.

that the beam of the vessel at the deck was correct. Once the forward futtocks were assembled and dogged down, the after futtocks (the other half of a double-sawn frame) were cut to length, assembled on top of, and clamped to the forward ones using them as a mold. Two trunnels were then driven between each futtock joint to hold the structure together. Finally a temporary cross spall (or crossbar) was nailed across the top of the frame to keep it from spreading.

Unlike the trunnels in the planking, which are cut off, split, and wedged inside and out, we usually just leave the trunnels for the frames long. With *Ardelle,* however, all trunnels were cut flush immediately. The reason for this was not structural so much as financial. Perry was using a rubber stamp she ordered on the Internet to emblazon the words "Pinky *Ardelle*" and our logo onto the square cut-off ends of every trunnel. She was then selling them as "Trunnel Tickets" (a ticket that would get you on a public sail after the boat was finished).

The most interesting part of the framing process for *Ardelle* came as each completed frame was stood up on the keel. This was when everyone could see her take shape and understand how each frame related to the one before. Moreover, as the frames lined up with the bevels true, the efforts of the modeler, the mold loftsman, the sawyer, the beveller, and the framing gang came together and the pride of everyone involved was evident.

Inset: Chuck R. boring a hole to bolt the cheeks onto the sternpost.

In the olden days when the frames were built on a platform that straddled the keel, the frames had to be stood up immediately so work on the next frame could commence. So as soon as each frame was completed, the head of the framing gang would cry out "Frame Up!" and everyone in the yard would drop what they were doing and help heave the frame into place. In the nineteen sixties our friend, the late Dana Story (Brad's Father), wrote a book called *Frame Up!* about old Essex and the shipyards. At the time, Dana thought he would never hear the echo of that cry in the Essex River Basin again. In a way he and his books were as important to keeping our history alive and our industry going as anything anyone ever did. When I watched

Left: Zack using a chain fall to hoist a forward cant up.

Above: Zack, Brian, Jim, Jeff, Pierre, Bob, Jim, and Harold putting a frame up forward.

the frames of *Ardelle* going up, I not only thought of it as part of a process but also a celebration of a tradition that spanned five centuries in Essex, a way of life, and a culture, that in spite of all the progress was not yet dead. So celebrate we did.

On Labor Day, 2010, the day after the Gloucester Schooner Festival, four or five hundred people showed up to sign *Ardelle*'s keel, wish us well, and help us to raise her first two frames in place. It was a beautiful day, and everyone had a great time. As summer turned to fall and fall to winter, Chuck, myself and a wonderful group of friends had a great time completing what we had started that day: building the remainder of the vessel's 32 frames, her centerline structure, and preparing her for planking.

During this time a lot more came together than the vessel's frame, and a routine developed. Chuck and I got started early, Chuck in the loft and I on the mill. Others would follow in to help with the heavy work as the day progressed. At ten we had a mug up and pastries that Steve or Dan usually brought and at twelve we had our noon meal, which started out as one-pot affairs that I cooked on the wood stove. Over time, though, these developed into elaborate meals: Steve brought fish, clams, and lobsters; Laurie's mother brought ham, beans, and cornbread; Kathy made chili, chicken soup, and all sorts of specialties, and many others contributed as well. As I could not afford to pay anyone it was nice that no one wanted to eat and run, and after lunch many people who had other things to do would stick around, and finish up what we had started in the morning. As the work tapered off most folks would disappear, Chuck would go back to the loft, and I to the mill until well after dark. In many ways the whole process felt like a barn raising with neighbor helping neighbor.

In the end while the advantages and disadvantages of using traditional heavy

Left: Zack cuts off the trunnels.

Above and Inset: Chuck (Harold's father), Harold, and Bernie Power shifting heavy bulkheads out of the barn.

Zack and Harold installing the keel bolts in the main hold.

construction techniques are arguable, I find the process and keeping the tradition alive particularly rewarding. Furthermore, I would say that there is a solid feel to a heavily constructed vessel that is hard to describe. Comparing this to the feel of a modern boat is not unlike comparing the way one feels entering a steel building on a cement slab to the way one feels entering an old timber-framed structure built into the side of a hill on a stone foundation, with bents, braces and pegs holding it together.

While they both may be equally functional, one feels like it is part of the element in which it stands and grew from the culture around it. And, that feeling is part of what we are trying to convey to our customers out on the water.

Steve Willard examines one of his cuts after he takes the clamps off of an assembled frame. Note the linseed oil and turpentine running out between the surfaces.

The whole gang struggles to carry the engine room bulkhead around the boat.

Inset: Harold temporarily clamps one frame to the next to make room on the aft deadwood to put up another frame.

Brian Chapski, Henry Szostek, Simon Koch, Jeff Lane, Jim Chambers, and John Drake lift a frame up onto the aft deadwood.

Harold drills a five-foot-long hole for a bolt in the after deadwood.

Harold planes ahead of Steve Willard who is fairing the hull with a belt sander.

Inset: Chuck Burnham caulking the bottom.

7

Planking

For many boat builders, myself included, planking is the favorite part of building a boat. It is the longest and most labor-intensive step in the process of building a vessel and doing it quickly requires a lot of people working together and coordinating their efforts.

Just after Christmas we finished the *Ardelle*'s frame and we celebrated this by nailing a small spruce tree atop her sternpost. Some have said this tradition harkens back to the pagan era and that the tree is put there to appease the gods. Others have said it is only parsimony, trying to stretch some more life out of something that should have been burned after the holidays. Whatever the case, Mother Nature was not appeased and she soon let us know.

A winter storm pounded the New England coast, producing a storm surge that flooded our boatyard and buildings with nearly fifteen feet of tide. Our shop—as well as the planer shed, band saw shed, and mechanical/electrical shed—were all flooded out. It also destroyed the pier where the *Maine* was tied. Thankfully, my friend Davis Griffith had a spare motor for the band saw, and while my father and I rebuilt the pier, Henry Szostek, our machinist, Geoff Richon from the Heritage Center, and my dad's friend Jack Kippen worked to get the planer fixed.

Once the planer was up and running again, it didn't stop for weeks. The Parkes boys and the whole gang carried the heavy planks down to the planer and ran them through the machine. This smoothed the rough sawn surfaces of the boards and brought them to a uniform thickness of about two inches. Once planed, the boards were then carried to the barn or back to the drying shed and sorted into piles of similar lengths and shapes.

While the planing was going on, Justin Ingersoll, a young shipwright who I had worked with in Maine, and Tim Walsh, a restoration carpenter, showed up to help Zack and me cut the rabbit. The rabbit is a notch or groove that runs the length of the keel and up onto the stem and stern-post into which the garboard (bottom) planks and the hood ends of the other planks are fastened. About this time Steve Willard, Bernie Power, and Bruce Slifer helped work the bugs out of our wood-fired steam generator and set up our steam box so that, by the end of January, we were ready to start planking.

The planking process started by "lining off," which is exactly what it sounds like. We took a black batten and nailed it to the frames to show where the tops of the streaks of planks would go. There was a lot to think about when lining off, not the least of which was that we had to end at the sheer or top plank. We thought about what stock we had available and how to best use that stock. We thought about the shapes of the planks and keeping them evenly tapered toward the bow and stern. We also thought about the shape of the boat and tried to keep the planks running with and not around the hard turns in the hull. Finally we thought about what the old-time Essex shipwrights told us about planking, which was to always "keep your lines straight and your hood ends up."

Like the frames, the planks for one side of the boat are mirror images of those on the other side, so we only needed to line off one side of the boat, which we did only a few planks at a time. Once this was done we then transferred the marks

Left: Steaming planks. After they are steamed it is important to get the planks hung while they are hot.

Right: Tim and Zack talking before mug up. Note the doughnuts, coffee, and mugs sitting on top of the hot steam box.

Following pages: Zack and Harold cutting the rab-bit in the keel in preparation for the garboard plank to go on. Note the sawdust-covered snow piled up on the forward face of each frame along the top of the keel.

indicating where the planks would go over to the other side of the hull so that both sides could be dubbed.

The term dubbing means using an adze, power plane, or angle grinder to fair the frames at the plank lines and then to put flats between the fair lines at the top of the plank and the next plank down. If the frames are dubbed properly, then each plank that is bent on will have one hundred percent contact with every frame. I don't know why the term dubber often has negative connotations, as dubbing is a skill that takes a good eye and some experience to master.

Although almost everyone had a hand in cutting the planks for the *Ardelle*, Justin did most of this work and he got quite proficient at it. Toward the end of the project he could get out four to six planks on a good day. While there is a lot to think about, cutting planks goes quicker than most people would think. As was said

The trunnels in this plank have yet to be cut, split, and wedged.

before, each plank is a mirror image of the one on the other side of the vessel, so we cut them out two at a time. The planks really don't have to be shaped so they fit the planks below, so much as cut fair. However, getting the widths, bevels, and seams correct is important. If these are done right, when the planks are steamed, they are easily edge set in place.

Before we steamed each plank for the *Ardelle* we coated each one with raw linseed oil and turpentine. This helped to keep them stable and gave them a beautiful patina. The steam not only made the wood more pliable, it helped balance out the wood's moisture content and hopefully killed any critters that might have been growing in it. Steaming wood was also a wonderful way of cleaning up the yard; Bernie and Steve burned the entire slab pile and several boats while steaming the planks for *Ardelle*.

After the planks had spent at least two hours in the box, the whole gang would pull them out of the box and "hang" them on the boat-clamping, wedging, and setting each plank in place. Next we fastened the hood ends, the setts, and the butts with a few bronze screws to hold the planks until they could be trunneled.

There was a lot to know about trunnels. Most importantly, a trunnel had to fit tightly in the hole that was bored for it. There is not a lot of tolerance between a trunnel that is so tight that it breaks off when you try to drive it or one so loose that it won't hold. It took some tinkering with our trunnel maker, which is not unlike a huge two and a half horsepower pencil sharpener, to get our trunnels sized to fit any particular auger. Once we got the size right, one man would make a batch of trunnels while another would go along and bore all the holes in the plank. Yet another man would follow along driving in the trunnels.

After the trunnels were driven, their ends were cut flush and split with a thin chisel. As soon as the chisel was extracted from the end of the trunnel, a wooden wedge was inserted and driven into the split end to keep the plank from pulling over it. On the inside of the boat, the trunnels that passed through both the plank and frame were finished in the same way as those outside. In a way these "through trunnels" are not unlike wooden rivets. "Blind trunnels," or those that do not pass through the frames but instead stop in the keel, deadwood, or floors, were handled differently. The inside ends of the blind trunnels were curfed on the bandsaw and a wedge was inserted into the curf before they were driven. This was done so that when the back of the wedge hit the bottom of the hole, it drove itself into the curfed end of the trunnel, spreading the trunnel in the hole in such a way that it could never pull out.

The trunneling on the *Ardelle* involved a lot of people. Bernie Power cut most of the seven thousand or so trunnel blanks. Henry and Eric Borden kept the trunnel maker working. Geoffry Richon made all of the fourteen thousand trunnel wedges. While just about everyone was involved in the making, drilling, and driving of trunnels, just about every trunnel was driven with a series of purpose-built wooden beetles (huge mallets) which Henry perfected through the process of making them.

On the *Ardelle* the caulking followed along about three streaks behind the planking, as it is supposed to. Although several people tried to help him, my father wound up doing most of this work, as he had done on other boats I built.

The caulkers are generally a separate group from the planking gang, but the rhythm of their mallets is ever present through the process and helps provide cadence to the whole operation. A good caulker can spread the tight seams with the material and tighten the loose ones by caulking on either side of them. Often times this will make the planking gang look better than they really are. Moreover, the cotton and oakum driven tightly into the seams makes the hull work as a unit against the racking and bending stresses from the ship moving in the waves.

Caulking takes extreme concentration and, when I caulk a boat, I find myself existing in the moment, far too caught up with the mallet, the material, and the iron to participate in any of the banter of the other shipwrights. At the same time, I find myself keenly aware of what everyone around me is saying and doing. The rest of the gang will often develop a healthy respect for the caulker, for although the caulker may not say too much, their rhythm makes a huge difference in the way the job proceeds and in the end, they keep the water out.

As we planked the *Ardelle*, winter continued pounding us with one storm after another but it did not really slow us down much. The steam box kept us warm and the snow piled up so thick it gave us a few streaks we did not have to stage for. By mid-April, winter was gone and we were hanging the last or, "whisky plank," and once again, it was time to celebrate.

After the seams are caulked they are painted with whatever paint is laying around.

Inset: Steve Willard forcing in the butt end of a hot plank.

Harold, covered in woodchips, pushes the hood end of one of the after planks into the sternpost rabbit.

The Ardelle's plywood deck going down.

Inset: Chuck Redman eyes the pattern for the gammon knee.

8

Decking, Painting, and the Launch

When the hull of a vessel is planked, it is only about half finished; however, I am a glass half full type of person. As soon as we recovered from the whisky plank festivities, Justin helped me get started making the patterns for, cutting, and installing the stanchions that support the rails and bulwarks. Soon after, Tim, Chad, and a number of other individuals joined in to help us out.

Steve Willard headed up the finish work. He started inside the boat, cutting and wedging all of the trunnels. Next he faired the inside of all the frames with a planer and a sander. When he was done, the frames looked so nice that we did the unthinkable and varnished them to show them off rather hide the rough frames behind the ceiling like we normally do. Now those massive frames with their trunnel fastenings are visible to all of the passengers, crew, and students who go below in the *Ardelle*. The sight of them gives everyone a sense of how ruggedly the *Ardelle* is built as well as how much the people who built her really cared.

Meanwhile, Bernie Power and Bruce Slifer laminated a new spruce main mast. To do this they used Epoxy donated by my friend Andy Spinney and his family business Anchor Seal Epoxy. Not only did Anchor Seal donate all the epoxy for the masts, but also for the bulkheads, deck, and the whole boat. This was a gift we not only appreciated but also are proud to have used. Andy, who has been my friend since

boyhood, has been involved in almost every boat I worked on, and we have been using Anchor Seal for over twenty years.

When they waited for the glue to dry on the laminates, Bernie and Bruce also helped me to cut the twenty-two, three-and-a-half-inch by four-inch deck beams, out of locust timber that I had been saving and drying for a long time. When we were through, Laurie Fullerton carefully varnished every one.

There was also a lot of metal work that needed to be done. Our friend Eric Borden helped us out with a lot of this. He made the patterns for the bronze pintle and gudgeon castings that would hold the rudder. Eric also got stock for and made the chain plate bottoms, hawse pipes, and the four-eyed "y" for the end of the bowsprit. Our friend Henry also helped out with a lot of this work, doing the machine work on the pintles and gudgeons once they were cast. Henry also helped to finish the chain plates and made the lower dead-eyes. Fran Cleary installed the gudgeons in the sternpost while Justin built the rudder and installed the pintles on it. The whole rudder assembly dropped together without a hitch when they were through.

The Ardelle's deck has been fiber-glassed, and the stanchions that support the bulwarks and rails have been cut in and reinstalled. Note the Maine in the creek stripped of her spars, engine, and deckhouses. Her deck houses are laying upside-down near the house, being prepped to be put on Ardelle.

When Chuck finished his work up in the sail loft, he put his artful eye to work building the gammon knee. This huge timber, which protrudes under the bowsprit, is largely decorative; its main function is to hold the carved trail boards. Though Chuck was just getting started in his boatbuilding career, no one could complain about the job he did. I can't walk, sail, or row past that piece of wood without giving it a prolonged lustful stare and I don't know whether I am prouder to be Chuck's teacher, friend, or the owner of the boat.

After Steve had finished up his work on the frames and Justin got the stanchions temporarily fastened in place, we scarfed together and bent in the heavy clamp shelf arrangement. The clamp shelf runs inside the sheer along both sides of the boat to stiffen her up, and gave us something to bolt the beams to. Once this was in place, the finished beams were then carefully cut, let into the clamp shelf, and bolted. With this done we then installed the carlines, the stud beams, and the mast partners in preparation for laying the deck.

Before the plywood for the deck could be laid down, Chuck carefully removed all the stanchions in order to avoid having to fit each piece of plywood over every stanchion. After the deck was installed and fiberglassed, each stanchion was carefully reinstalled into holes cut for them in the deck. A laminated plywood deck goes down much faster than a traditional wooden one, but laying it is a miserable task. As was often the case with the *Ardelle*, my friends were quick to lend a hand when I needed them. Mike Dyer, Laurie Fullerton, Davis Griffith, Bernie Power, Bruce, Chad Gadboise, Steve Willard, Chuck Redmond, Zack Teal, Jeff Lane, Paul Schwartz, and a few others all helped with this process. Together we cut all the plywood, varnished the bottom of the first layer, nailed it down, glued and nailed the second layer, and fiberglassed the whole deck in less than a week. With this mammoth task behind us we were really in the home stretch and the gang of people that kept showing up to help just kept growing.

Holes were soon cut in the deck, the stanchions installed, the pinky stern built, the bulwarks and cap rails went on forward, the bowsprit was fit and rigged, the main mast was finished up, and the foremast and deck houses were salvaged from the *Maine*. To be honest, though, what I remember most about the next few weeks of building the *Ardelle* was how tiring and demoralizing I found it, trying to stay ahead of Steve Willard as we faired the hull together.

Somehow, I survived and about two weeks before the event we announced a launch date. There is a natural curiosity that tends to bring every person who enters the yard while we are building a boat to ask, "When are you going to launch her?" Although this question seems innocent enough, it invariably triggers the stress of the thousands of challenges that lie between the time they ask the question, and the

Above: Harold fairing the bottom.

Inset: Harold, his daughter Perry, and her friend Cole Neugebauer.

Above: Ardelle, half faired and primed.

Right: Dick Sleeper paints the rudder.

event of their curiosity. Because of this, we never set a launch date until we know we can reach it, and we generally respond to anyone asking by gritting our teeth and saying, "She will launch when we are ready." That is, up until we set a date. For the *Ardelle* her launch was finally set for July 9, 2011.

With the launch less than a few weeks away, there was still much to be done. The launch date helped to mobilize more and more people to drop whatever they might have had planned and help us finish the boat. Thankfully, while everyone who worked on *Ardelle* was volunteering, many of the crew that showed up in the last few days were people who had helped me launch my previous four schooners and the whole process went like clockwork. Justin and Chuck took over the work on the rails, Francis put the lead flashing around the stem and bowsprit, Bob Brophy worked on the carvings, Bernie Noon and John Miles filled in the pine bulwarks, Henry and Zack installed the chain plates, Davis showed up and helped build the breast hook, Ben Lower and Pierre built the sheet horse, and countless people showed up to help

Four days before launch.

Steve paint and putty her. We got the boat ready the night before the launch, took the stage down, and on the morning of the ninth we got things ready under the boat.

Although they only happen every few years, our launchings are the largest events that happen in Essex these days, and draw a crowd that often exceeds the population of the town. Some people feel that the reason so many people show up to watch our launches has to do with the fact that we build our boats out in the open in the center of town where everyone can watch them come together. Others say it has to do with the town's deep connection to the shipbuilding industry. My friend Bob Hicks credits the huge turnouts to an "aura of uncertainty." All of these possible reasons, however, are encompassed in the traditional method we use to launch our boats.

This method is referred to as an Essex side launch. It is called this not because the vessel slides sideways into the water, but instead because the vessel slides into the water on its side. While this method was once common in Essex and Gloucester,

Ardelle in the early morning on launch day. Note the staging is gone and the boat is ready to go.

H.A. BURNHAM
DESIGNER · BUILDER

I have not heard of it being used elsewhere, even though it is relatively cheap and simple to set up. To set up for the launch we first build a single way or " bilgeway" under one bilge, and cover it with grease. Next we lean the vessel over so that its bilge rests on a "car" (or short plank and wedges) that lays on the bilgeway. Then with the vessel leaned over, starting aft and working forward, we drive greased pine slabs up under the keel while we split out the blocking on which the vessel was built. At some unknown point, gravity overtakes friction and we have a launch. Interestingly, the slope of the bilgeway is generally steeper than the slope of the keel, so the vessel rolls down during her descent. At the point when she strikes the water, she is on her beam ends. With any luck at all, the buoyancy of her quarters will float her stern, keep her from tripping, and carry her through the shallows at the river's edge.

As the afternoon of July ninth rolled on, we set up the bilgeway and prepared the slabs to be driven up under the keel. Just before high tide, Perry and Laurie broke a bottle of champagne against *Ardelle's* stem, we lowered her onto the bilge rail and Zack climbed aboard. Finally, we cut the chain that held her and starting aft and

Below: Harold under the boat, getting ready for launch. Note the heavy chain running to a dead man, set up to avoid a premature launch.

Right: The hawser hanging from the hawse pipe is attached to a heavy drag to keep the Ardelle from drifting off once she is afloat.

Left: We have a launch.

Right: The gang who helped us get her ready on launch day poses for a picture after our midday meal.

working forward, wedged the slabs up under her keel and split the blocks out from under her.

As I split out the last block, the *Ardelle* creaked for a second, started to slide aft, and then just stopped. While other boats have taken some jacking to get them moving, I just knew she was going to go. I put a jack against her and gave it a couple of clicks and as she started I leaned into her. Then as they realized what was happening, a number of friends jumped in to help push, and off she went.

Because the slope of the bilgeway is steeper than the angle of the keel, the vessel rolls down during the decent so that she strikes the water on her beam ends.

9
Fitting Out

After the launch, we tied *Ardelle* on our mooring in the middle of the river and took a week off before towing her into the creek beside the shop to get started on making her ready for her maiden voyage. There was a lot left to do. Justin and Henry made a tiller. Zack and I installed the engine and systems. Bruce and Henry fit out the spars. Steve Willard and Mike Dyer installed the hatches we had salvaged from the *Maine*, over the forecastle, main, and aft holds. Paul Schwartz made new hatches for the engine room and aft deck. Chad installed the windlass. Alden and his grandfather, Lovell, built the deck boxes. Chuck made ladders and built the chalk rails. Simon Koch and Jose M. Hernandez-Juviel installed the standing rigging. And dozens of people showed up to paint, clean up, or help in any way they could.

We took our first trip under power on August first; it was a hot day and we thought it a good time to try the old engine we had salvaged from the *Maine*. We headed down river and everyone went for a swim. The next week Geoff Richon brought his crane over from Gloucester and installed the masts. By the following week we had her all rigged up, ballasted and sailing.

After passing a stability test we did for the Coast Guard we brought her out the river and around to Gloucester on August twenty-third. We started out fairly

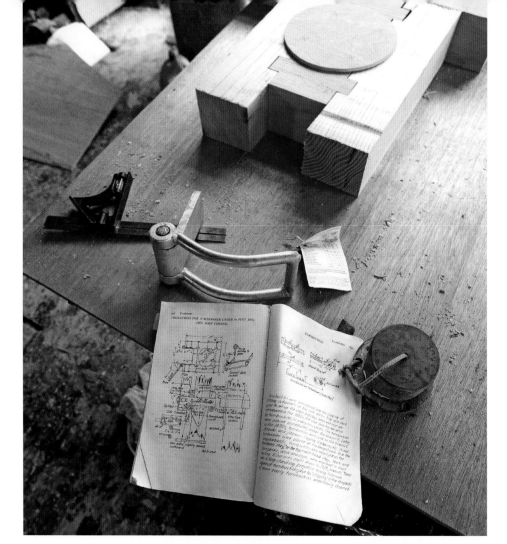

Left: A copy of Chappelle's American Fishing Schooners.

Right: Harold, Zack Teal, and Bruce Slifer working on the sketch for the mast head.

Inset: Spars in the shop on horses.

early in the morning in light airs and stopped in Rockport for lunch. By mid-afternoon we had a good breeze and as *Ardelle* sailed up Gloucester Harbor for the first time, she was accompanied by our friends the Ellis's aboard their schooner *Thomas E. Lannon* which we had built for them fourteen years earlier. When she approached her home at the Gloucester Maritime Heritage Center, hundreds of people had gathered to welcome her. The crowd included State Senator Bruce Tarr, who exclaimed to the crowd, "This schooner is really about our heritage—about who we are."

Just under a year after we laid the keel for *Ardelle* we finished construction, did our drills, received our Coast Guard certification, and ran our first public sail on September 2, 2011. This brought an end to one of the most rewarding and humbling experiences I have ever had. Looking back, I am astounded that we were able to pull it off, and all I can feel is gratitude toward my family, my friends, and my community who made it possible.

Above: Harold, Bruce Slifer, and Chad Gadbois installing the windlass.

Inset: Jeff Lane and Harold guide the heel of the fore mast into place.

Right: Simon Koch signals to Geoff Richon in the crane as Harold guides the mast through the partners.

While I can never repay them, I do try to take everyone who helped build the boat sailing as often as I can. They have joined me on public sails, I have given them private charters, and every year we reserve the Mayor's Cup Race during the Gloucester Schooner Festival for our building crew and their guests.

Over the years we have taken *Ardelle* on "busman's holidays" all over the coast of Maine and Massachusetts. In the fall of 2012, I was honored to receive a National Heritage Fellowship (the Nation's highest honor in the traditional arts) from the National Endowment for the Arts for my work keeping the shipbuilding traditions alive in Essex. A number of the gang who helped me build her, also helped me to sail her down to Washington D.C. to pick up the award, and I am hopeful that someday I will be taking her a lot further than that.

Below left: The galley.

Below right: The crew's quarters in the aft hold.

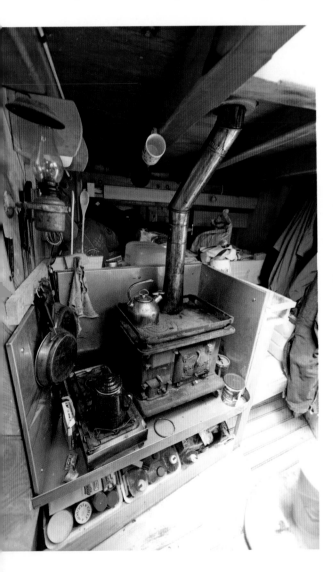

Inset: Bob Brophy carves the hailing port the day before the launch.

Below: John Miles and Bernie Noon installing the pine bulwarks the day before the launch.

Above: Mast hoops hung up in the shop.

Inset: Bernie Noon bending a mast hoop over a form.

Right inset: The deadeyes and standing rigging were salvaged from our old schooner Maine.

Right: The blocks hung up to be varnished.

10

Sailing

Besides the "busman's holidays" and the many trips we have made with family and friends the *Ardelle* has proved a busy little workhorse indeed. Since her completion, we have consistently run over three hundred trips a year on her out of the Heritage Center in Gloucester, helping them inspire students and visitors to learn about marine science maritime heritage, and environmental stewardship.

Through our public sails and charters, locals, tourists, artists, and rusticators of all types have been able to experience some of our culture, feel our heritage, and see our natural resources from the perspective of an authentic indigenous working craft. In addition to unique weddings, family reunions, and memorial services, we have hosted scientists, musicians, poets, artists, and historians to share their knowledge of our place and culture with all who join us.

As far as education goes, to date we have taken nearly 10,000 students sailing. In the Ocean Explorers program alone, we have taken over 1,500 students from every third, fourth, and fifth grade class on Cape Ann (including the communities of Essex, Gloucester, Rockport, and Manchester) out sailing, hauling lobster traps, working with NOAA scientists, and conducting marine science investigations each year since the boat was built.

Inset: Ardelle's box compass was salvaged from the Maine.

Below: Sailing with much of the building crew in the Mayor's Cup Race during the 2011 Gloucester Schooner Festival.

Sailing up Eggamogin Reach in Maine on a "busman's holiday."

While we can never repay those many folks who helped us and continue to support us, we have done our best to give back by helping to support Maritime Gloucester, the Essex Shipbuilding Museum and many other local charities, donating charters and hundreds of "trunnel tickets," to worthy causes.

Over the years we have also put a lot back into the *Ardelle*. Bruce Slifer built out her interior. We have upgraded her safety equipment and installed hydraulic steering

and a new engine. Now, not only is she ready to go anywhere, but I am comfortable allowing capable captains to take her out when I cannot.

One of the things that I am most proud of is that the *Ardelle* has been very good for the young people who work and sail on her. Several of our crew are well on their way to seagoing careers. All of the money she has made selling beer and wine has gone to my kid's education fund. My daughter Perry is now studying Management and Organizational Leadership at Emmanuel Collage, and my son Alden is studying History and Education at Boston University, and recently passed his captain's exams.

Zack, who helped so much while the *Ardelle* was under construction and rode her on her initial plunge, is at the Maine Maritime Academy and has just passed his exams for Mate on vessels up to two hundred gross tons.

In the end, I should mention that as far as shipbuilding and our Essex yard goes, although the *Ardelle* is all the boat I want or need, John Abazaid has not stopped dropping off logs and over the winters I have not stopped milling them into timber. So sooner or later I guess I am going to have to find a use for all of that wood.

Acknowledgments

I n August 2012, building a vessel for my family was something I had dreamed about for a long time. I had been making preparations to begin building the *Ardelle* for over a year. At that point, however, I secretly hoped that, someone would either hire me to build them a boat which would take precedence over my own or, at the very least, try to talk me out of it. Instead what my friends, family, and community offered was encouragement, support, and no excuses.

While there are far too many people who helped make this project a reality to thank them all individually, I feel I must mention some. I should start with my father, who not only inspired and encouraged me to build boats, but also allowed me to use his tools, without which I would have never gotten started. My mother, brother, sister, aunt, and many cousins also deserve a lot of credit for their help, support, and encouragement, in this project, and in many other projects like it. I would like to thank all of them for allowing me to use our family shipyard. Like many a family farmer I consider it an honor and privilege to live here and to keep this place going for everyone to enjoy.

As for the project's funding, I thank the Massachusetts Cultural Council who gave me an artist grant, which I used as seed money and the National Endowment for the Arts for the honorarium they gave me with the National Heritage Fellowship which helped pay off some of the debt. I also must thank the many friends and family that kept the project going between those grants, after the money that I had saved from my early seagoing career was long exhausted. You know who you are, and I really could not have done it without you.

My friend David Wyman set the *Ardelle*'s pay scale for everyone involved. As a professional engineer, David helped me with several past design projects. When I asked him about helping me with *Ardelle*, he said he would under the condition that he not be paid.

The late Harriet Webster, Geoffrey Richon, Steve Parkes, Amanda Madeira, Mary Katharine Taylor, and all the folks at the Gloucester Maritime Heritage Center deserve a great deal of credit, not only for helping with the *Ardelle*'s creation, but also ensuring she would have a home berth and an educational mission when she was completed.

Chuck Redman, my apprentice, signed the keel on Frame Up day saying his "heart and soul is in this boat." I sometimes call him from ports afar to joke with him about where we've taken his "heart and soul," but it's no joke that the *Ardelle* is a better boat for having them. I do not think I could have built her without his help and the help of the regular crew who worked with us.

Some of that regular crew included, in no particular order, Steve Willard, Bernie Power, Pierre Erhard, Andy Spinney, Charles Burnham, Dave Brown, Davis Griffith, Simon Koch, Chad Gadbois, Steve Parkes, Alex Parkes, Matt Parkes, Robin Tattersall, Steve Hastings, Justin Ingersoll, Justin Demetri, Bernie Noon, Bill Blackwood, Aaron Snider, Fred Ebinger, Dusty Clampitt, Jack Fialowski, Kirk Williamson, Tom Hastings, Jose M. Hernandez-Juviel, the Cronin Family, Ben Lower, Phil Burns, Jackson Friedman, Tom Ellis, Geoffrey Richon, Daisy (the toothy dog), Jeff Lane, Len Burgess, Nancy Dudley, Tim Walsh, William Redding, John Miles, Mike Rutstien, John Symonds, Eric Borden, Henry Szostek, Bruce Slifer, Bob Brophy, Jim Chambers, Francis Cleary, Jim Aaron, Mike Dyer, Owen Brown, Brian Chapski, Dick Sleeper, the Drakes, the O'Brien's, Louis Maffei, Jim Witham, and countless others whom I apologize for omitting.

Zack Teal, the youngest regular member of the building crew, deserves a special thank you. He and his parents convinced his school of the value of the project and they allowed him to intern on the boat one day each week, which including the weekends, put him on site three days a week. And although his parents and I were continually reprimanding him for using tools and equipment he wasn't supposed to, his youthful energy and enthusiasm did much to fuel the whole project.

Speaking of fuel, I should mention Kathy Slifer, the Fullerton family, Maria Burnham, the neighbors at Burnham Court, and the many folks who did not work on the boat, but helped the crew in oh so many ways, from bringing food and pastries

for the many fantastic coffee and lunch breaks we shared, to putting up with noise into the night and so much more. It was truly amazing.

One neighbor, The Essex Shipbuilding Museum, deserves recognition for organizing the Frame Up event, the Launching, as well as interpreting the project to visitors and running tours and educational programs throughout the entire construction.

My own kids, Alden and Perry, also deserve a special thank you. They had to live it. In addition to her help with the paint and putty, at the Frame Up event and launching, Perry worked hard helping with the business plan and selling trunnels, planks, t-shirts, and knick-knacks from her Snug Harbor Gift Shop to keep things going. While Alden was striving toward his own independence as we built *Ardelle*, through the process he learned a lot about his family, his heritage, and a truly unique way of life. We are both grateful to his grandfather, Lovell, for encouraging him to help build the deck boxes and pleased that Alden survived the ordeal to work as crew on *Ardelle* sixty-plus hours a week once we got the boat operational.

Finally, I must thank Laurie Fullerton for all that she did. This included helping with the press, working on the boat, and promoting the *Ardelle* during the construction. She also helped me get the business started in its first year of operation and much more.

—Harold Burnham,
Essex, Massachusetts